INSIDE THE WORLD OF SPORTS

INSIDE THE WORLD OF SPORTS

AUTO RACING
BASEBALL
BASKETBALL
EXTREME SPORTS
FOOTBALL
GOLF
GYMNASTICS
ICE HOCKEY
LACROSSE
SOCCER
TENNIS
TRACK & FIELD
WRESTLING

INSIDE THE WORLD OF SPORTS
FOOTBALL

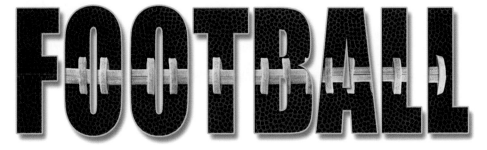

by Andrew Luke

MASON CREST

Mason Crest
450 Parkway Drive, Suite D
Broomall, Pennsylvania 19008
(866) MCP-BOOK (toll free)

First printing
9 8 7 6 5 4 3 2 1

Names: Luke, Andrew.
Title: Football / Andrew Luke.
Description: Broomall, Pennsylvania : Mason Crest, [2017] | Series: Inside the world of sports | Includes bibliographic references, webography and index.
Identifiers: LCCN 2015046929| ISBN 9781422234600 (Hardback) | ISBN 9781422234556 (Series) | ISBN 9781422284223 (eBook)
Subjects: LCSH: Football--United States--History--Juvenile literature.
Classification: LCC GV951 .L85 2017 | DDC 796.330973--dc23 LC record available at https://lccn.loc.gov/2015046929

QR CODES AND LINKS TO THIRD-PARTY CONTENT

You may gain access to certain third-party content ("Third-Party Sites") by scanning and using the QR Codes that appear in this publication (the "QR Codes"). We do not operate or control in any respect any information, products, or services on such Third-Party Sites linked to by us via the QR Codes included in this publication and we assume no responsibility for any materials you may access using the QR Codes. Your use of the QR Codes may be subject to terms, limitations, or restrictions set forth in the applicable terms of use or otherwise established by the owners of the Third-Party Sites. Our linking to such Third-Party Sites via the QR Codes does not imply an endorsement or sponsorship of such Third-Party Sites, or the information, products or services offered on or through the Third-Party Sites, nor does it imply an endorsement or sponsorship of this publication by the owners of such Third-Party Sites.

CONTENTS

KEY ICONS TO LOOK FOR:

Words to understand: These words with their easy-to-understand definitions will increase the reader's understanding of the text while building vocabulary skills.

Educational Videos: Readers can view videos by scanning our QR codes, providing them with additional educational content to supplement the text. Examples include news coverage, moments in history, speeches, iconic sports moments and much more!

Text-dependent questions: These questions send the reader back to the text for more careful attention to the evidence presented there.

Research projects: Readers are pointed toward areas of further inquiry connected to each chapter. Suggestions are provided for projects that encourage deeper research and analysis.

The Vince Lombardi trophy has been awarded to the winner of the NFL Championship at the end of each season since 1967. It was first presented as the Vince Lombardi trophy in 1971 when it was renamed for the Green Bay Packers' coach following his death. A new trophy is made every year as the winners keep permanent possession of the trophy after they receive it on the field.

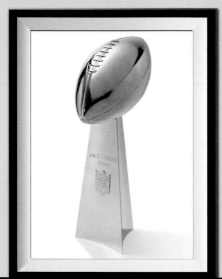

CHAPTER 1

FOOTBALL'S GREATEST MOMENTS

By far the most popular game in America, professional football, as embodied by the National Football League (NFL) brand, dominates the sporting landscape. In 2015, the Super Bowl was the most-watched program in U.S. television history, with more than 114 million viewers. This allowed rates for the 2016 game to be set at a record $5 million for a 30 second ad, generating more than $350 million for broadcaster CBS.

Football's popularity lives far beyond the boundaries of its signature event. On a weekly basis from September into January, fans flock to stadiums across the country to watch their local teams compete. This is no passing fancy. In Green Bay, the Packers have a waiting list for season tickets. There are more than 100,000 names on it. The list continues to grow as new parents add the names of their babies as soon as the ink dries on the birth certificate. Those babies will be 30 before they get near the top.

Twenty-four of 32 teams currently have a wait list for season tickets, but the popularity of NFL football is perhaps best encapsulated by the tradition of tailgating, that is, eating and drinking in parking lots off the tailgate of your vehicle.

It is almost a sacred ritual at some stadiums, where fans arrive hours before the game to demonstrate camaraderie with their fellow supporters. In Cleveland, Ohio, for example, fans arrive at 7 a.m., even for games that do not start until 8 p.m.

In Kansas City, fans stage homemade BBQ sauce competitions. In Philadelphia, strangers welcome each other over hot grills in September and hot tubs in January. Every game is an event, celebrated with gusto by loyal fans.

Ticketless fans hold similar celebrations in each other's homes every week, gathering to feast together and watch games on TV, from preseason to playoffs, and especially for the Super Bowl.

Three generations of Americans have grown up watching the NFL Championship on television. Since the first coast-to-coast broadcast in 1951, the game's most significant moments have unfolded in living rooms across the country.

The Immaculate Reception

Entering the 1972 Divisional Playoffs, the Pittsburgh Steelers had never won a playoff game. A play in their game against Oakland changed that—and the fortunes of the franchise, and of the NFL, forever.

The Steelers trailed the Raiders 7-6 with just 22 seconds remaining in the game. On a fourth-down play, Steeler quarterback (QB) Terry Bradshaw tossed the ball in the direction of halfback John Fuqua at the Raider 35-yard line. Raider safety Jack Tatum closed to make a play on the ball as it approached Fuqua.

The two players collided, and the ball deflected in the direction of Steeler running back Franco Harris, who reached down and is ruled to have made a fingertip catch off his shoestrings, barely an inch off of the ground. Harris ran it all the way into the Raider end zone, and the Steelers won the game 13-7.

The Hail Mary

Hail Mary is a term that once referred to any offensive play that had little chance of success. Named for the prayer, it traces back to Notre Dame in the 1920s.

That reference changed during the 1975 National Football Conference (NFC) Divisional Playoff game between the Dallas Cowboys and the Minnesota Vikings. The Cowboys trailed 14-10 with just 32 seconds remaining in the game. The Cowboy offense, led by QB Roger Staubach, had the ball at midfield. Staubach took a snap and then threw deep right. Cowboy wide receiver Drew Pearson caught the ball on the 5-yard line. He walked into the end zone for the game-winning touchdown.

After the game, Staubach joked with reporters that he said a prayer as he threw the pass, adding, "It was just a Hail Mary pass. A very, very lucky play." Now, the term Hail Mary is widespread and refers to desperation, last-second, long-distance pass plays.

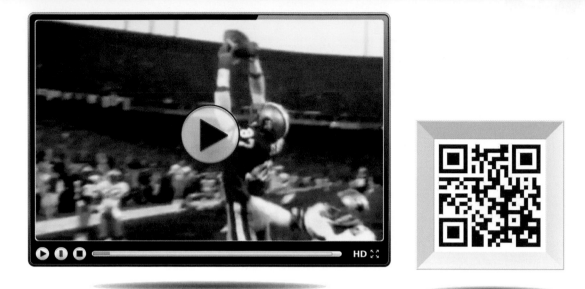

The Catch

The legend of Joe Montana began on January 10, 1982. The San Francisco 49er QB was playing in his second playoff game, facing the Dallas Cowboys in the NFC Championship Game.

The score was 27-21 Dallas when San Francisco got the ball with less than five minutes left in the game.

Montana drove to the Cowboy 6-yard line. It was third and three with 58 seconds to play. After the snap, Montana threw high to the back of the end zone.

Tight end (TE) Dwight Clark was under the sailing ball, and he outleapt cornerback (CB) Everson Walls with a full-extension stretch to make a fingertip catch, now known as The Catch. The touchdown gave San Francisco the 28-27 lead with 51 seconds left. The Niners held on to win.

Perhaps the most significant impact of The Catch occurred off the field that day. Sitting in the stands at Candlestick Park watching that game and cheering for his hero Montana was four-year-old Tom Brady.

Watch the video instantly on your mobile device by scanning the QR code next to each video player!

The Drive

Expectations were as high as possible for QB John Elway when he was the first overall pick in the 1983 entry draft. He began to live up to those expectations in the American Football Conference (AFC) Championship Game against the Cleveland Browns. In that game, Elway led his team on "The Drive."

The Drive began on Denver's 2-yard line with the Broncos behind on the scoreboard 20-13 and 5:32 to play in the game. Elway moved 98 yards through the stingy Browns defense, capping The Drive with a 5-yard strike to wide receiver (WR) Mark Jackson with 39 seconds left.

The game went to overtime, and the Elway-led Broncos offense, brimming with confidence, moved the ball 60 yards on its first possession to set up the winning 33-yard field goal.

Elway went on to his first Super Bowl, and although the Broncos did not win that game, he would go on to win two of his five Super Bowl appearances.

Wide Right

Elway's fellow 1983 first round draft pick, Buffalo Bills quarterback Jim Kelly, played in four Super Bowls of his own. Kelly's Bills also lost their first Super Bowl game, but it was the manner in which they lost that might have scarred that team forever.

At Super Bowl XXV, the Bills faced the New York Giants. New York led 20-19 with 2:16 on the clock. Kelly put together a tough drive, and with 8 seconds left in the game, the Bills were on the Giant 29-yard line, which meant Buffalo's Scott Norwood had a 47-yard field goal attempt to win the Super Bowl.

The pressure was too much for Norwood, and his kick veered, "Wide right!", the now-famous call from TV commentator Al Michaels as the ball missed.

The Bills made the Super Bowl the next three seasons but were beaten badly in all three tries. That one-point loss is as close as they have ever come.

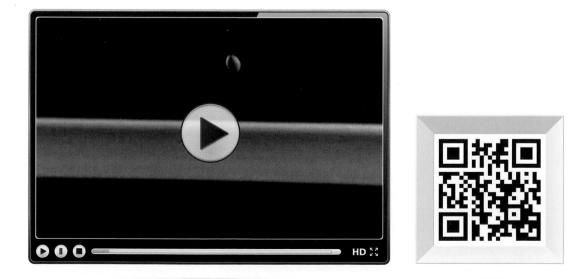

The Music City Miracle

Hard-luck playoff results for Buffalo were not confined to Super Bowls, however. In the 1999 wild card playoff round, the Bills faced the Tennessee Titans in Nashville, Tennessee, aka Music City. This time, after a field goal, the Bills led by a point, 16-15, with only 16 seconds left.

That's when Titan fans will say divine intervention occurred. On the ensuing kickoff, Titan running back (RB) Lorenzo Neal received the kick. Running a designed play called "Home Run Throwback," Neal lateraled to TE Frank Wycheck, who then threw an overhand lateral all the way back across to the left side of the field. Titan WR Kevin Dyson caught the ball and ran 75 yards down the sideline for the win.

Buffalo has missed the playoffs every season since. The Titans, on the other hand, used the game as a springboard to advance all the way to that season's Super Bowl.

One Yard Short

Super Bowl XXXIV featured that same Titans team against the St. Louis Rams, the NFL's dominant offensive team. The Rams' offense was known as the Greatest Show on Turf.

It was a tight game, and with 6 seconds left and the Rams leading 23-16, the Super Bowl victory came down to the final play.

At the snap, Titan QB Steve McNair fired a quick pass to Dyson at the Rams' 5-yard line. Rams linebacker Mike Jones was waiting. Dyson took two strides before Jones wrapped him up and started to drag him down. Dyson extended the ball in a valiant effort to get it over the goal line, but he famously came up one yard short.

This game was the high point for each franchise. The Rams returned to the Super Bowl two years later but lost to Tom Brady's Patriots. Neither team has won a playoff game since 2004.

Watch the video instantly on your mobile device by scanning the QR code next to each video player!

The Helmet Catch

Speaking of the Patriots, it would be difficult to get through this list without an entry from the franchise that has gone to eight Super Bowls. In six of those, the team was led by Tom Brady, that same four-year-old who watched Dwight Clark make The Catch and grew up to be a four-time Super Bowl champion.

Coming into Super Bowl XLII, the Patriots were undefeated, facing a 10-6 New York Giants team.

Trailing 14-10 with 1:15 remaining, Giants QB Eli Manning threw the ball down the middle of the field, where WR David Tyree, an unsung special teams player, was able to grab the ball and hold onto it while falling by pinning it against the top of his helmet with one hand. The play preserved the drive, which ended in the game-winning touchdown to Plaxico Burress four plays later. The Giants knocked off the mighty Patriots 17-14.

Words to Understand:

derivation: the source or origin of something

rugby: a game in which opposing teams try to carry or kick a ball over the other team's goal line

scrum: a way of starting play in rugby in which players from each team come together and try to get control of the ball by pushing against each other and using their feet when the ball is thrown among them

CHAPTER 2

THE ORIGIN OF AMERICAN FOOTBALL

It is difficult to pinpoint just how the version of football we enjoy in America evolved. Most experts believe it came from rugby, which in turn is a **derivation** of the game the rest of the world calls football: soccer. Some say that to trace soccer's origins, we need to go back to the ancient days of Greece and Rome. Other experts even believe the Chinese played some form of soccer as many as 2,500 years ago.

THE BARE-BONES BEGINNING

The most commonly held theory, however, is that the game evolved in England around the year 1050. The story is that workmen digging in a field on which battles had been fought with Danish invaders came upon the bones of the fallen, including skulls. The English held a lot of bad feelings toward the Danes, who occupied England for more than 25 years earlier that century. The workmen took out this anger on the skulls and kicked one of them back and forth across the field. A group of boys passing by witnessed this and began to play with another of the skulls, calling the game Kicking the Dane's Head. As most of the boys were barefoot, however, kicking the skull was painful, so the boys evolved to playing with an inflated cow bladder.

Using the bladder as the object of play made for a much a better sport as it could be kicked harder and went further. The game spread from town to town, and teams were formed, and matches were contested. When the king, Henry II, heard of the newly popular sport, he banned the game because it was taking away from the popularity of archery. The ban lasted well into the 13th century before reemerging in a form similar to modern-day soccer.

A HANDS-ON VERSION

About 300 years later, the Irish invented what they called Gaelic Football, the game we now know as **rugby**. In Gaelic Football, players could pick up and handle the ball, running with and throwing it as needed, which was strictly against the rules of soccer. Gaelic Football was given the name rugby in 1823 by William Ellis of Rugby College.

THE BOSTON GAME

In America, both rugby and soccer had come over with the colonists and were popular games. The first organized college soccer game in America is believed to have been between Princeton and Rutgers in 1869. But by 1871, students at Harvard University had grown tired of the rules of soccer and developed modifications, which they called the Boston Game. This version allowed players to pick up the ball and run with it and had 15 players per side. They believed this version to be so much better than soccer that they declined to participate in an 1873 convention that was held to formalize rules for intercollegiate soccer games.

Group photo of an unknown early American football team

Looking for competition for the Boston Game, Harvard's players looked outside the U.S. border to Montréal. In 1874, they played the Boston Game against a team invited from McGill University. Further rule modifications made the Boston Game look even more like rugby, with an oval ball and rugby-style tackling. Also like rugby, if a tackled ball carrier did not immediately release the ball, a **scrum** was deemed necessary by rule. This also applied if the ball went out of bounds. Also similar to rugby, the scrum involved placing the ball between the two teams and then having the linemen fight for possession. When the team from McGill arrived, they only had 11 players, so both sides fielded that number of players.

CAMP RULES

The Boston Game modifications brought some elements of what we know as football today, but it was still closer to rugby than anything else. And rugby was losing its luster as well. In 1880, disenchanted by the rules of his sport and what he believed to be its disorderly play, Yale University rugby captain Walter Camp decided to make some changes. Camp created a distinct line of scrimmage with the teams facing each other but with only one designated

Walter Camp

to control possession of the ball. However, an issue arose with there being no limit to the length of possession. Teams could control the ball until they scored or fumbled, making the games low scoring and, in the eyes of spectators, dull. Case in point is a game between Yale and Princeton in New York the following year. Ten thousand spectators watched, but no one scored. Princeton held the ball for the first half, Yale for the second, and everyone yawned throughout.

This debacle prompted suggestions to improve the game. The first incorporated by Camp was to implement the concept of downs; teams had three plays in which they had to give up possession if they at any point lost ten yards or after the third play had failed to gain five yards. Fields were subsequently marked with chalk at 5-yard intervals.

The rugby scoring system also was not to Camp's liking. A touchdown did not gain any points, rather simply the opportunity to get points via a free kick field goal. Safeties existed but also yielded no points. He believed the touchdown itself should be a scoring play and that safeties should be rewarded on the scoreboard as well. In 1883, he introduced his new scoring system, where touchdowns were worth two points and safeties a single point each. A kicked goal following a touchdown became worth four points, with field goals themselves worth five. By 1912, the scoring in place was as it stands today: six points for a touchdown, one point for a conversion, and three points for a field goal.

A MODERN TOUCH

Camp, the father of American football, headed the sport's rules committee for 25 years, creating the positions on offense: seven linemen, a quarterback, two halfbacks, and a fullback. He devised game plans and play signals. Many aspects of the modern game were added after Camp's time, however. He was against huddling, and linemen could not even crouch, much less put their hands on the ground. He did not particularly like the forward pass, so while it was allowed, it was severely restricted. Passes could not exceed set distances, and incomplete passes were ruled to be turnovers. This changed in 1906 when majority rule forced Camp to adopt more lenient passing standards. The distance to keep the ball on a set of downs was changed to 10 yards, and the rule of keeping the ball if a team lost 10 yards was removed.

Other rule changes followed over the years. The field was shortened to 100 yards from 110, helmets became mandatory, and goal posts were moved from the goal line to the back of the end zone.

The first professional league, the American Professional Football Association, was formed in 1920, and Camp's creation began to take hold in some areas of the country. Football was in its infancy, but there were a lot of growing pains to come in the years ahead.

Text-Dependent Questions:

1. What was "Kicking the Dane's Head"?

2. Who is known as the father of American football as he is credited with creating the sport?

3. When was the first professional league created?

Research Project:

Do an online scavenger hunt to find artifacts that represent the origin of football. Locate images and articles showing and describing the game, players, old uniforms, equipment, and so on. Share your findings by creating an online blog or scrapbook. Get the ball moving!

Sammy Baugh

CHAPTER 3

THE FIRST PROFESSIONALS

This new form of football spread in popularity in turn-of-the-century America, catching on at colleges in the Northeast as well as with local athletic associations in several cities. Games between neighborhood teams became the most attended events in town once the baseball season ended.

The difference was that these city association teams paid players to compete, while college players, just like it is in today's game, would lose their eligibility if they took money to play. Despite this fact, in an age without the Internet and instant photo sharing, many college players were paid to play using false names.

PAID IN PITTSBURGH

The first known example of a professional player was in Pittsburgh, Pennsylvania. Two club teams, the Allegheny Athletic Association (AAA) and the Pittsburgh Athletic Club (PAC), played to a 6-6 tie on October 21, 1892. They quickly scheduled a rematch for three weeks later to settle matters. With both teams determined to win at any cost, each side took to trying to recruit college players illegally.

Pudge Heffelfinger was an All-American who played guard for Yale. He was approached separately and secretly by both the AAA and the PAC and eventually played in the rematch for Allegheny. On a snowy November day, Allegheny won 4-0 when Heffelfinger scooped up a Pittsburgh **fumble** and returned it 25 yards for the game's only score. Accusations of professionalism flew back and forth, and all wagers on the game were eventually canceled. It was not until 70 years later that the discovery of an old Allegheny account book revealed that Heffelfinger had been paid $525 to play in the game.

THE SPREAD OF PROFESSIONALISM

In 1895, professional players came out of the shadows for good. The local YMCA in Latrobe, Pennsylvania, just east of Pittsburgh, paid high school QB John Brailler $10 to play for them. Toward the end of the 1895 season, Latrobe played rival Jeanette. Every player on both teams was paid $10 in what is considered to be the first all-professional game.

Jim Thorpe

This phenomenon began to occur across the Midwest. Players were paid on a per-game basis with payments coming directly from ticket sales. There was, however, indefinite free agency. Players were lured to play for different teams each week. There were no contracts, and there was no team loyalty. In-game fights and high-stakes gambling were frequent and gave the sport a black eye.

One famous example comes from 1906, when prior to a game between nearby Ohio rivals Canton and Massillon, Canton hired four Massillon players away to come and play for them instead. But Massillon won the game anyway, sparking accusations that the players switching teams was part of the Massillon plan all along, and they had conspired to throw the game. This marked the end of football in Canton for a five-year span.

THE EARLY SUPERSTARS

Football was revived in Canton in 1911. By 1915, Jack Cusack was managing the Canton Bulldogs team. Cusack, the man who later brought the Pro Football Hall of Fame to Canton, received national attention that year when he signed Olympic Games hero Jim Thorpe to play for $250 per game. Thorpe was a household name, having won two track and field gold medals for the United States at the 1912 Olympics in Sweden. Fans flocked to see the superstar, who is widely considered to be the greatest American athlete of the 20th century. Thorpe, who was of Native American heritage, attended university at Carlisle Indian Industrial College in Carlisle, Indiana. There, he excelled in football, baseball, lacrosse, and track and field. Under the **tutelage** of coach Glenn "Pop" Warner, Thorpe was a football All-American in 1911 and 1912, leading Carlisle to the national title in 1912, including a famous upset of powerhouse Harvard.

Thorpe's presence swelled attendance at Canton games from 1,200 to 8,000. This eyebrow-raising success led to other superstars joining the professional ranks. This included University of Notre Dame standout Knute Rockne. Rockne had graduated from Notre Dame after his playing days and was assistant coach of the team in 1915. He would coach the Irish on Saturdays and then travel to Ohio to play for Massillon on Sundays. Rockne would go on to lead the Irish to four national titles before being killed in a plane crash and is widely credited with bringing the forward pass to the game. He led Massillon to the championship that year.

THE FIRST PRO LEAGUE

When the American Professional Football Association (APFA) formed in 1920, Thorpe was named president. The league saw many peaks and valleys in the early years of existence. Aside from Chicago, and Detroit, the 10-team league existed in relatively small towns, where it struggled to survive. The first-ever APFA game featured the Rock Island Independents from Illinois versus the St. Paul Ideals from Minnesota. The Independents won 48-0. The Akron Indians won the first championship, going undefeated that season.

The league, however, lacked organization. Teams made their own schedules and played as few or as many games as they liked. Thorpe lasted only one year as president, and his replacement, Joe Carr, made some changes. Carr started with the name, rebranding the association as the National Football League. He also was dedicated to establishing the league in big cities. The Chicago team was renamed the Bears to capitalize on the popularity of the city's baseball team, the Cubs. In New York, Tim Mara paid the league $500 for a franchise and named his team the Giants, also piggybacking on the name of that city's baseball club.

The Bulldogs were the league's early dynasty, winning 24 straight games from 1922 to 1923. In 1923, their opponents scored a total of 19 points for the entire season. Lou Smythe was the league's biggest star. He is the only player ever to lead a team in both passing and rushing touchdowns in a season. Despite their success on the field, Canton was like many small-town teams in that they were not profitable. They moved to Cleveland in 1924.

THE COMPETITION ARRIVES

The first appearance of the American Football League (AFL) came the next year, 1925. A league of this name would play a very significant part in football history more than 30 years later. This version of the AFL, however, formed around another superstar, Harold "Red" Grange. Known as the Galloping Ghost, Grange was a three-time All-American halfback at the University of Illinois. In his career there he rushed for more than 3,300 yards in just 20 games and scored 31 touchdowns. He became a national star in a 1924 game when he scored six touchdowns against favored Michigan. After he graduated in 1925, NFL teams hotly pursued him. But Grange and his agent had a different idea. They arranged to play with the Bears but only for an exhibition tour. The tour was a huge success, and Grange earned $100,000. So when the Bears made Grange an

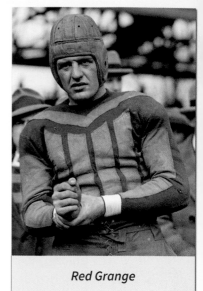

Red Grange

offer to play with team for the 1926 regular season, he refused, realizing he had an opportunity to cash in further on his popularity. Grange and his agent started the AFL with nine teams. Grange played with the New York team, predictably named the Yankees.

The two leagues battled for public attention. In 1926, the NFL allowed franchises to anyone who asked and could pay, and the league grew to 23 teams. In the major cities, both leagues were represented, and neither could win a majority of fans. At AFL games, other than those featuring Grange, attendance was dismal. Many teams went bankrupt, and only four were left at the end of the season. The NFL did little better. In New York, for example, a Giants versus Bears game drew only 83 paying fans. Only 11 teams survived the season.

IMPROVING THE GAME

Competition was not the main problem for pro football, however. The game itself had major flaws. From 1920 to 1932, nearly two-thirds of the game included one team that did not score any points. The rules of the game favored the defense and coaches employed **conservative** field position strategies. They often would punt on third down, for example. Passing was discouraged. Quarterbacks had to drop back at least 5 yards to throw, and end zone incompletions were considered turnovers. Scoring was difficult. Even field goals were challenging after the goal posts were moved to the back of the end zones in 1927.

To open up the offense, the NFL turned to Bears owner George Halas. Known as Papa Bear, he ran the team for more than 60 years. He was the most influential owner. Rule changes had no hope of adoption without his blessing. He believed in star power, entertainment, and marketing. And although his championship teams of the 1930s and 1940s were built around rushing and defense, he was a big proponent of opening up the passing game, which was the springboard that caused the NFL to thrive.

Text-Dependent Questions:

1. The first known example of a professional player was in Pittsburgh, Pennsylvania. What was his name?

2. In 1915, Jack Cusack was managing the Canton Bulldogs team. He received national attention that year when he signed Olympic Games hero Jim Thorpe to play for how much money per game?

3. The first appearance of the American Football League (AFL) came in what year?

Research Project:

Do some investigating online to find the current salaries of players in different positions and on different teams today. Then look back at how the salaries for various positions progressed over the years since the first player was paid $525 for a game back in 1892.

Controversial today for its racially offensive nickname, the Redskins played in Boston for five seasons before moving to Washington D.C. in 1937.

Words to Understand:

antics: attention-drawing often wildly playful or funny act or action

unprecedented: not done or experienced before

concede: to give away something usually in an unwilling way

CHAPTER 4

RISE OF THE QUARTERBACK

In 1936, the Green Bay Packers met the Boston Redskins in the NFL Championship Game. This was supposed to be a home game for the Redskins, but there was so little interest in the game in Boston that it was moved to a neutral site in New York instead. It is the only NFL Championship Game pre-Super Bowl to be played at a neutral site, and the game had a huge effect on the future of the league.

LEAVING BOSTON BEHIND

The Redskins were owned by George Preston Marshall, a fact that was bringing him no joy at the time. The team was $90,000 in the red, and he had tried desperately to change its fortunes. In moves that would meet with serious controversy in today's society, he hired a Native American to coach the team and ordered the players to wear historical Native American war paint on their faces during games. Boston also fielded a marching band at halftime, the first team in the league to do so. Yet still, no one came to the games, despite the **antics** and even despite winning records. Marshall made no secret of the fact that he was looking for a new home for his team.

Boston lost the championship to the Packers 21-6. The announcement that the team was leaving Boston for Washington, DC, came three days later. Marshall had identified a lack of star power on his team as a major concern. He had some great players, as this was after all a team that just played in the championship game. The roster that year included future Hall of Fame players RB Cliff Battles, WR Wayne Milner and tackle Turk Edwards. Marshall, however, felt he needed more than merely great players. The country was mired in the Great Depression, and he needed more than great to convince fans to part with their precious dollars. He had to have a superstar.

SLINGIN' SAMMY BAUGH

Enter Sammy Baugh, a college quarterback playing at Texas Christian University (TCU). Marshall heard the buzz on Baugh during business trips to Texas. Baugh had earned the nickname Slingin' Sammy for his prowess as a baseball player, but it easily could have been due to his penchant for throwing the ball 20 to 25 times in football games. This was more than double the pass attempts a team of that era would typically take. And Baugh was not just throwing a lot, he was throwing it on target and deep, even on first down. Baugh also served as the team's punter, a job at which he also excelled. It was reported famously that he had honed both skills back home in Sweetwater, Texas. He threw footballs through the center of a tire swing and kicked them in the air, attempting to land them on a rag placed 50 yards away.

Originally built in 1930, Amon G. Carter Stadium has hosted TCU football games through three expansions and a major renovation in 2010.

Baugh's ability to throw the ball was **unprecedented**. TCU games were attracting upwards of 80,000 fans in 1936, Baugh's senior year. Marshall knew he had to have Slingin' Sammy to jump-start his first season in Washington. The next year, 1937, was the second year of the NFL draft, and Washington had the sixth pick in the 10-team draft. Typical of the times, three running backs and a center were picked ahead of Baugh. There was, however, a quarterback that went ahead of him as well. The Chicago Cardinals decided they had a need at the position as well but went with Buzz Buivid from the relatively nearby Marquette University. Marshall was able to draft Baugh and promptly offered him the league's largest salary, $8,000.

Baugh did not disappoint. The Redskins won the 1937 season opener 13-3 over the Giants behind 116 passing yards from Baugh. He threw 16 passes, with 11 completions and five drops. Not once did he miss a receiver. Word of his performance spread, and fans packed not only his home stadium but road stadiums as well to get a glimpse of Slingin' Sammy. Sold-out crowds watched all season long as the rookie led Washington to that season's NFL Championship victory.

Baugh was an unassuming superstar—humble, witty and easygoing. His popularity with fans, teammates, and media alike was unsurpassed. He signed autographs for fans for hours after games and gave freely of his time for public appearances and teaching kids the passing game.

PASS HAPPY

Baugh was exactly what George Halas was hoping for. The success of Baugh's style of play gave Halas the ammunition he needed to convince his colleagues that this was the time to release the defense and run-first mentality that shackled scoring in the league. "Every rule was against making you want to throw the ball," Baugh said. "I thought it was a very conservative game. But after my first year, more teams started passing the ball. They finally realized that people like to see scoring. You don't want to sit out there in the cold and see a 14-6 game."

Halas, along with Marshall, supported rule changes to increase passing, including a rule to protect the quarterback from being hit after the whistle was blown. "It was the silliest rule you ever saw," Baugh said. "Sometimes those linemen would chase the quarterback 20 yards, and the ball would be 70 yards away with the guy running with it. Mr. Marshall asked me if I thought it would help the passing game if they came up with a rule that said the quarterback couldn't be hit after the play was blown dead. I said, 'Sure, it'll add a few years to his life.'"

Sammy Baugh changed football forever. His popularity was as high as that of any sports star in America, including Joe DiMaggio and Ted Williams. Kids now wanted to be quarterbacks as much as they wanted to be baseball sluggers, and coaches began to look for kids who had the ability to excel at making passing a key part of the game plan.

In 1943, Baugh had the greatest individual day ever recorded in the league. He threw four touchdowns, intercepted four passes (players still played both offense and defense), and averaged 52 yards per punt.

Baugh set more than a dozen punting and passing records. He still has the record for seasons leading the league in passing yards with six. He also led the league in punting four times and is second in career punting average. He won a second NFL Championship in 1942 and was a seven-time All-Pro.

Don Hutson

STAR POWER

Baugh was the biggest star in the game through the 1940s, but he certainly had peers. In Green Bay, Don Hutson was the most highly regarded receiver in the league. The Packers star came out of the University of Alabama in 1935 with a reputation for being a deep threat. He could run the length of the field in under 10 seconds. Halas famously remarked about Hutson, "I just **concede** him two touchdowns a game and hope we can score."

Hutson went 83 yards on his very first NFL catch and never looked back. In 11 seasons, he caught 488 passes, including 99 touchdowns. Hutson was versatile, also serving as the team's kicker. Against the Lions in 1944 Hutson had the greatest quarter any player has ever had in the history of the league. He scored four touchdowns and kicked five extra points. Those 29 points scored is still the current NFL record. Hutson's Packers won three championships, and he retired as the greatest receiver the game had yet seen.

The best running back of the era was Chicago Bear standout Bronko Nagurski. His battering ram style led the Bears to championships in 1932, 1933, and 1943. Nagurski grew up on a farm in International Falls, Minnesota. He was recruited to play for the University of Minnesota by coach Clarence Spears. Spears was the architect of the first building block to the legend of Nagurski, inventing the story of how when he arrived at the Nagurski farm to meet Bronko, he was plowing a field without a horse. Nagurski's legend grew as he plowed through college defenses as a fullback for the Gophers from 1927 to 1929.

When Nagurski went to play for Chicago in 1930, he was 6'2" and 230 pounds, a size that even today would be impressive for a fullback. In the 1930s, he was a giant. Nagurski was often bigger than most defensive players, and his size and strength are illustrated in a famous story about a touchdown he scored against the Redskins. On this run, two linebackers came up to make the tackle, and he knocked them in opposite directions. Next came a cornerback who Nagurski pounded to the dirt before smashing through a safety while going into the end zone. He then bounced off the goalpost into the brick wall of Wrigley Field. Returning to the huddle, legend has it that he said, "That last guy hit me awfully hard."

Nagurski demanded a $6,000 salary for the 1938 season. The Bears declined to pay, so Nagurski retired and went on to a career as a professional wrestler, where he starred until 1960. He did play the 1943 season with the Bears as there was a shortage of players due to World War II. He led them to the championship victory and then promptly retired for good.

As Nagurski was leaving the Bears, he crossed paths with the other great quarterback of the era, 1943 teammate Sid Luckman. Luckman came to the Bears out of Columbia University in 1939, and he and Baugh were rivals throughout the 1940s. In the four seasons between 1940 and 1943, Luckman and Baugh met in the championship game three times. Luckman's Bears won twice, including the 1940 game, where the Bears ran the score up to 73-0.

The week prior to that 1940 game, Redskin owner George Marshall made public comments about the Bears, including calling them crybabies, quitters, and losers. The Bears were not amused and took it out on Marshall's players on the field. The score should have been worse than 73-0, actually. As the Bears scored so often, the officials ran out of footballs and had to order that no more extra points be kicked. They completed the game with an old practice ball. Luckman ran for one touchdown and threw for another of the Bears' 11 in the most lopsided game in NFL history. When asked if a dropped pass in the end zone that he threw early in the game had made a difference, Baugh said, "Sure. The final score would have been 73-7."

The Luckman-led Bears scored a ton in the 1940s in an offense that was spread out in a T formation. His greatest individual game was in 1943 when he threw for a then-record 443 yards and seven touchdowns. Luckman won four NFL Championships and was a five-time All-Pro.

CHANGING OF THE GUARD

With the success of the offenses led by Baugh and Luckman (six championships in a 10-year span), the T formation supplanted the single wing as the most-used offensive set, and the aerial attack on defenses was underway. By 1946, all teams had adopted the T, with the exception of the Pittsburgh Steelers. At that time, the war had just ended, and stars like Baugh, Hutson, and Luckman had kept interest in the league high during a difficult time for the country. This era provided the platform on which the NFL would build the most popular sports league in America.

Text-Dependent Questions:

1. Who is known for his penchant for throwing the ball 20 to 25 times in football games, which was more than double the pass attempts a team of that era would typically take?

2. In 11 seasons, which receiver caught 488 passes, including 99 touchdowns?

3. Which star player retired and went on to a career as a professional wrestler after the Chicago Bears wouldn't pay him a $6,000 salary in 1938?

Research Project:

Research the average career length of players in the NFL, and compare what positions have the shortest and longest careers. Create a digital presentation to share this information with your class in an exciting and engaging format.

Paul Brown Tiger Stadium is a high school football stadium located in Massillon, Ohio.

Words to Understand:

momentous: very important, having great or lasting importance

cemented: made certain

viability: the capability of succeeding

CHAPTER 5

SEGREGATION, THE SHIELD, & SUPER BOWLS

The years following World War II were a prosperous time in U.S. history. Postwar America was booming, and this prosperity was reflected in the spread of professional football.

COMPETITION AND DESEGREGATION

In 1946, the All-American Football Conference (AAFC) was formed, which included the San Francisco 49ers and the Los Angeles Dons, the first pro teams on the West Coast. In response, the NFL moved the Cleveland Rams to Los Angeles to compete with the Dons. The AAFC countered by putting a team in Cleveland, which was named the Browns after head coach Paul Brown.

The addition of the Browns was another **momentous** event in league history. Brown revolutionized coaching at the pro level. He hired full-time assistant coaches. Players were subjected to IQ tests to determine if they were able to follow his difficult schemes. He packaged all the team's plays into playbooks and held off-field, classroom-style meetings where the playbook was the text. He measured the 40-yard dash ability of his players and studied film of his team's performances postgame to determine which players were excelling and which needed more work. Brown also had substitutes take new plays into the huddle. All of these elements are still employed in some form by NFL teams today, and their introduction changed the game.

Brown was also the first coach in the modern (postwar) era to voluntarily sign African American players. Thirteen African Americans are recorded to have played in the NFL from 1920 to 1933, from Fritz Pollard to Ray Kemp. But when Kemp quit to pursue a successful coaching career in 1933, Washington owner George Marshall, who entered the league in 1932, pressured his colleagues to segregate the league. He openly refused to have black players on his team and was successful in keeping them out for more than a decade. This included blocking an attempt in 1940 by George Halas to sign University of California, Los Angeles (UCLA) phenom RB Kenny Washington.

PAUL BROWN

One of the most influential coaches in history, Paul Brown introduced playbooks and film study and championed integration as well.

That changed when the Rams moved to Los Angeles. They were forced to sign a black player so that they could get a lease to play in the Coliseum. The city would not allow a lease to a segregated team. The Rams found Washington playing in the minor leagues and signed him in April 1946. That gave Brown the opportunity to follow suit. He added future Hall of Famers RB Marion Motley and guard Bill Willis in August of 1946. With the color barrier broken in both leagues, all teams, with the exception of Marshall's Redskins, soon had black players.

The Browns also signed Northwestern University star QB Otto Graham in 1946. Graham and Brown combined to lead Cleveland to all four AAFC championships before the league folded. The NFL absorbed three AAFC franchises: the Browns, 49ers, and Baltimore Colts. The merger did not slow Graham and the Browns down. They reached the NFL Championship game each of the next six seasons, winning in 1950, 1954, and 1955, Graham's last season. He retired having reached the championship game in every season he played, winning seven titles. His .814 career winning percentage is still an NFL record for starting quarterbacks.

COURTING TELEVISION

Brown never won another championship in the 15 years he coached after Graham retired, but his legacy as a game changer was **cemented**. The league itself, however, still lacked financial stability.

Tasked with solving the league's revenue problem, NFL commissioner Bert Bell looked to increase television revenue. At the time, most teams were broadcasting their road games back to their local markets, and there were some nationally televised games, but televised football on Sundays was rare. Bell needed a catalyst to convince the networks that his product should be a regular programming feature nationwide. On December 28, 1958, he got one.

THE GREATEST GAME EVER PLAYED

On that day, the Giants played Baltimore in the NFL Championship, a game that was televised nationwide. The game has been labeled "The Greatest Game Ever Played," but had you been one of the 30 million viewers watching in 1958, you might not have agreed come halftime. The Colts led 14-3, and the Giants offense had been dormant all game. Baltimore was driving for another score in the third quarter that would surely have clinched a victory. That's when the fortunes of NFL football on TV changed forever.

The Giants stopped the Colts and then staged a furious comeback to take a 17-14 lead, but Baltimore tied it at 17 with 7 seconds left to force overtime.

The Giants got the ball first but failed to score. Baltimore took possession on their 20-yard line, and QB Johnny Unitas led another brilliant drive. In 12 plays, he led his team to the New York 1-yard line. TV viewers were just as enthralled as the 64,000 in attendance—and then . . . nothing. Fans watching at home saw nothing on their televisions, which went black right before the play from the 1-yard line. Furious, viewers scrambled to become listeners, searching for their radios. At NBC, the broadcasters were in an equal frenzy trying to get the signal back. An intoxicated fan wandering onto the field was enough of a delay for technicians to reattach a cable that accidentally had been kicked loose, and the picture returned just in time to watch Alan Ameche run the ball in for the winning score. That drunk fan on the field? He was neither drunk, nor a fan, but rather an NBC employee sent out to stall as needed.

THE AFL RETURNS

For weeks, the 23-17 Colts' win was the talk of the country. Johnny Unitas was the new end to that sentence on the lips of every boy who declared, "When I grow up I'm going to be . . ." Football was in the national spotlight, and for once it was the NFL, not the NCAA game garnering all the attention. Advertisers noticed. The networks noticed. And Lamar Hunt noticed.

Johnny Unitas

Hunt was an oil millionaire who decided he wanted a piece of the pro football action. He tried to bring a franchise to Dallas, but that move was blocked. Undeterred, Hunt revived the American Football League, keeping the name from 1925. Hunt's version of the AFL did significantly better. ABC bought five years of rights to televise AFL games, ensuring the league would be stable.

Flush with cash, the AFL franchises in Boston, Buffalo, Los Angeles, New York, Dallas, Denver, and Houston bid strongly against the NFL for players. The two leagues competed throughout the decade, eventually agreeing to have an interleague championship game beginning in 1967.

SUPER BOWLS AND MONDAY NIGHTS

The 1967 AFL–NFL Championship was held at the Los Angeles Coliseum. Led by then three-time All-Pro and four-time NFL Champion QB Bart Starr, Green Bay lived up to its billing, winning easily 35-10 over Kansas City. The Oakland Raiders suffered the same fate the following year as the AFL representative, losing 33-14 to Starr and the Packers.

Following the second noncompetitive game, experts questioned the **viability** of making the matchup a tradition, saying the AFL was not of the same caliber as its more established rival. That theory would again be put to the test in the third game. The AFL New York Jets played the Colts in Miami, Florida, in what is now called Super Bowl III. This was actually the first game, however, to be called the Super Bowl officially. Hunt had been referring to the game by this name from the beginning, but it was not adopted until 1969.

The Jets were heavy underdogs to the Colts, even though Unitas was injured and had not played all season. Brash young Jets QB Joe Namath, however, had his own ideas. Three days before the game at a public appearance in Miami, he stirred the pot by guaranteeing a Jets win. Namath then went on to deliver a 16-7 victory that stunned the NFL and changed the way the public viewed the upstart AFL.

The two leagues finally merged formally before the 1970 season. ABC came to the table with a big-money deal to broadcast games, including moving one featured game to prime time on Mondays for Monday Night Football. With unprecedented TV exposure, growth exploded. By 1978, polls showed 70 percent of sports fans said they followed the NFL, as opposed to only 54 percent who followed baseball.

TELEVISION AND RADIO FACTS

More than 500 television stations and 550 radio stations will broadcast the NBC Television and Radio Network's coverage of the third AFL-NFL World Championship game, Sunday, Jan. 12.

In the United States the colorcasts will be carried by 215 stations, including (on a delayed basis) stations in Alaska and Hawaii.

NBC International has arranged for the network coverage to be fed to 265 Canadian stations and 20 stations in Mexico. The more than 550 radio stations which will carry the game will include 250 stations in the United States. In addition, the Armed Forces Radio and Television Service will beam the broadcast world-wide via shortwave to its more than 300 radio outlets in the Far East, Pacific, Latin America and Europe. Kinescopes of the NBC-TV coverage also will be sent to many AFRTS television stations around the world.

The television line-up, with the Miami area blacked out, will cover 98.8 per cent of the television homes in the United States while the radio line-up will cover 100 per cent of the radio homes.

Eleven color cameras will be used for the NBC coverage, as opposed to a normal five to seven for a regular season professional game.

Game time for NBC Television and Radio is 3 p.m. EST. The NBC-TV Network will televise a pre-game program at 2:30 p.m. EST, NBC Radio at 2:45 p.m. EST.

NBC Television commentators: Curt Gowdy, Kyle Rote, Al DeRogatis.

NBC Radio commentators: Charlie Jones, George Ratterman, Pat Summerall.

NBC Television producer: Lou Kusserow; director, Ted Nathanson.

NBC Radio producer: Parker Gibbs

AFL-NFL WORLD CHAMPIONSHIP GAME

Third World Championship Game

PRESS GUIDE/AFL VS NFL

GROWING PAINS

Growth came with its share of issues, however. There were three player strikes between 1974 and 1982 as the players sought to increase their slice of a growing pie. On the owner's side, many sought greener pastures by relocating franchises. Five franchises moved between 1982 and 1995. Performance-enhancing drugs (PEDs) plagued the game in the 1970s and 1980s. In 1987, the league had to initiate a banned substances policy that now includes not only PEDs but illegal street drugs as well. Since 1987, the NFL has suspended more than 225 players for failing drug tests, which are issued randomly under the policy.

The turn of the century saw even greater prosperity for the NFL. By 2002, there were 32 NFL teams. It is by far and away the most popular sports league in North America. Average annual attendance at NFL games is more than 17 million people. That is nearly 70,000 people per game, more than any other sport in the world.

PROTECTING THE SHIELD

Along with growing exposure, the league also had a growing image problem. A disproportionate number of its players had run-ins with the law. In 2006, nine members of the Cincinnati Bengals were arrested in nine separate off-field incidents. Issues like these prompted NFL Commissioner Roger Goodell to establish a personal conduct policy in 2007. Goodell claimed it was his job to "protect the shield," referring to the league's shield design logo, by preserving the NFL's public image. The league continues to suffer bad publicity from players being charged with everything from spousal abuse and dog fighting to drunk driving, manslaughter, and murder.

On the field, the issue of brain injury due to concussions became high profile when former players sued the NFL over how these injuries had affected them. The NFL settled by creating a $675 million fund for injured players. Goodell also enacted rules and policies designed to reduce on-field concussions and identify concussed players more readily.

Despite these issues, the league's popularity is soaring. TV rights have greatly expanded. The NFL partnership with all four major networks is worth more than $40 billion. The league also makes billions in sponsorship deals with several companies from PepsiCo to DirecTV.

The NFL has a multibillion-dollar licensing division that allows for merchandise from T-shirts to trash cans bearing team logos to be sold.

The Dallas Cowboys franchise won three Super Bowls in the 1990s and today is worth more than $3 billion. Three other franchises are worth more than $2 billion. Every NFL franchise is among the top 50 most valuable sports franchises in the world.

While improvements in the game itself, like adding the two-point conversion in 1994, have certainly made it a more watchable and popular product over the years, the one thing that has remained a constant driver of interest and attraction and continues to put the NFL at the forefront of American sports is superstar players.

Text-Dependent Questions:

1. In 1946, which conference was formed with the first pro teams on the West Coast?

2. What happened to cause TV viewers to see nothing but a black screen right before a big play from the 1-yard line during the 1958 NFL Championship?

3. How many player strikes were there between 1974 and 1982 as the players sought to increase their slice of a growing pie?

Research Project:

Look back at the past 20 years of televised football games, and make a spreadsheet to detail the ad revenue that various TV networks have collected over the years during broadcasted games . . . most notably the Super Bowls.

Drew Brees

Words to Understand:

marquee: headliner players

reins: control or power

incumbent: currently holding a position, role, or office

CHAPTER

MODERN-DAY STARS

From way back in the days of Red Grange, the NFL has relied on the star power of its **marquee** players to drive the popularity of the sport.

This continues to be true into the 21st century. Stars can raise the profile of franchises from one of local interest to that of national headliner, and nowhere is this more evident than at quarterback.

THE SIGNAL CALLERS

The pass-friendly modern game has made quarterbacks the biggest stars in the league. There are exceptions, but generally, it is the franchises with the superstar quarterbacks that have the most success. At the turn of the century, a crop of quarterbacks drafted within seven years of each other made their mark on the league.

Aaron Rodgers was the last of this crop to be drafted, coming out of the University of California at Berkley after his junior year in 2005. The first round of Rodgers draft is often

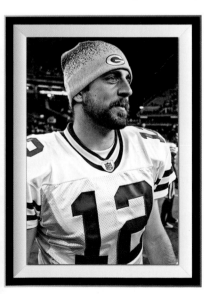

Aaron Rodgers

talked about as one of the most dramatic ever. Rodgers was thought to be a consensus number one pick, which was held by the 49ers. But San Francisco took Utah QB Alex Smith instead, and Rodgers fell all the way to 24th, where Green Bay selected him.

Rodgers backed up future Hall of Famer Brett Favre for three seasons, finally taking the **reins** in 2008 and instantly becoming one of the best quarterbacks in the league. In his first 10 seasons, he won two NFL MVP awards, went to four Pro Bowls, two as an All-Pro, and won Super Bowl XLV, where he was voted MVP. Rodgers led the Packers to the playoffs in seven of those 10 seasons. He has the lowest interception percentage and the highest quarterback rating in league history.

Drew Brees

Cam Newton

At only 6 feet tall, Purdue quarterback Drew Brees was smaller than model modern-day quarterbacks like Rodgers. San Diego took a chance on him with a second round pick in 2001. But the Chargers never fully believed in him, sitting him behind veteran Doug Flutie for 21 of his first 43 games with the franchise. They then drafted QB Philip Rivers in the first round after his fourth season. Despite going to the Pro Bowl in 2004, the Chargers still let Brees go to New Orleans as a free agent after five years.

Brees thrived in New Orleans, where he blossomed into one of the best quarterbacks of the modern era. He never threw for fewer than 4,000 yards with the Saints. He went to eight more Pro Bowls, was named All-Pro three times, led the league in passing yards five times, and won Super Bowl XLIV as the MVP. Brees is top five all-time in career passing yards and touchdowns.

Unlike Brees, Auburn University quarterback Cam Newton was highly touted when he was the first pick of the 2011 draft by Carolina. At 6'5", scouts were attracted to his size and then fell in love with his ability to both pass from the pocket and make athletic plays with his legs.

In his 2011 rookie season, Newton had a spectacular first game, setting the record for passing yards in a debut, a record that was held by Otto Graham for 61 years. Newton went on to break the rookie QB records for passing yards, rushing yards and rushing touchdowns. Newton was named Rookie of the Year, but he had his best season in 2015, winning league MVP after leading the league in touchdowns. He also led the Panthers to the Super Bowl. Newton holds the NFL record for career rushing touchdowns by a QB.

At the opposite end of the spectrum from a high profile first overall pick like Newton is Tom Brady. The New England Patriots drafted Brady in 2000. He was almost an afterthought, taken with pick number 199 in the sixth round. He barely made the Patriots roster as the fourth-string quarterback.

Brady's obscurity dissolved the following season. He had become the backup to starter Drew Bledsoe and came into the Patriot's second game of the year after Bledsoe was badly injured. That was the beginning of a Hall of Fame career. Brady led the Patriots to the playoffs that season and all the way to the Super Bowl, in fact. Brady was named MVP in a 20-17 win over the St. Louis Rams.

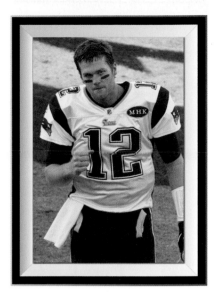

Tom Brady

Brady rocketed to stardom, winning three more Super Bowls and two more Super Bowl MVPs. He holds several career playoff passing records and is a two-time NFL MVP. When Brady and main rival Peyton Manning played each other on the field, the games were featured events. Early in their careers, Brady's Patriots dominated Manning's Colts, winning the first six matchups, including two playoff games. After that, the results were more equal, with Manning winning two AFC Championship Games against Brady.

Off the field, the two stars could not be more different. Manning married his college sweetheart. Brady's love life was often tabloid fodder as he dated actresses and married Brazilian supermodel Giselle Bundchen. Manning got all the endorsements, while Brady got the headlines. On the field, however, Brady was the more accomplished superstar. Many believe he is the greatest quarterback of all time.

THE BALL CARRIERS

Another testament to the greatness of Brady is that he never played with a great running back. Last century was the heyday of the running game in the NFL, and, therefore, that is when most of the great running backs played. There have, however, been some great halfbacks in this millennium as well.

The 2008 NFL draft produced a couple of standouts at running back, but neither of these was picked in the first round. Tulane University's Matt Forte was actually the fifth running back selected that year, chosen by Chicago in the second round. Of the four running backs picked in the first round, none made the Pro Bowl. Forte has played in two.

Forte is not only a threat running the ball, but he is the most versatile back in the game because of his ability to catch the ball out of the backfield. No running back in history has ever caught as many passes in a season as Forte did in 2014 with 102.

DeMarco Murray   *Jamaal Charles*

The eighth running back taken in 2008 was third-round pick Jamaal Charles, going from the University of Texas to the Kansas City Chiefs. There, it took him just six years to become the leading rusher in Chief history, despite losing almost all of the 2011 season to a knee injury. A track star in college at Texas, Charles has tremendous breakaway speed. He used this to his advantage on a spectacular 91-yard touchdown run against New Orleans in 2012.

In 2010, Charles rushed for 1,467 yards on only 230 carries, just a hair shy of Jim Brown's yard-per-carry record of 6.4, set in 1963. He averaged a very impressive minimum of at least 5 yards per carry in each of his first seven seasons. Charles has played in four Pro Bowls and has been All-Pro twice.

In the following draft year, the best running back in the 2009 class was once again not picked in the first round. The Philadelphia Eagles picked LeSean McCoy in the second round, and once again, neither of the running backs picked in the first round ever played in a Pro Bowl. McCoy played in three, two of those as an All-Pro. He led the league in rushing touchdowns in 2011 and in rushing yards in 2013.

McCoy played only two seasons at the University of Pittsburgh before going pro and spent his rookie season behind **incumbent** starter Brian Westbrook. With McCoy's emerging talent evident, the Eagles released Westbrook and "Shady" (a childhood nickname that stuck) stepped in, carrying the ball at least 200 times every season and gaining 1,000 yards in all

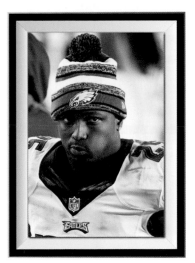

Matt Forte   LeSean McCoy

but one. After the 2014 season, the Eagles made the surprising decision to trade McCoy to Buffalo. They felt they had the opportunity to upgrade from their All-Pro-caliber back.

That upgrade was 2011 draft class member DeMarco Murray. Murray entered the league with the Dallas Cowboys out of Oklahoma University. The Cowboys selected Murray in the third round, and his first three seasons were decent enough. Then came the 2014 season.

In 2014, Murray had one of the best seasons ever for a running back. He racked up 1,845 rushing yards, 17th best in NFL history, to lead the league. His 392 carries were the seventh most all time. That was enough for Philadelphia. Murray was a free agent after his All-Pro season, and Dallas would not meet his price. The Eagles got rid of one All-Pro to bring in another.

THE PASS CATCHERS

With the explosion of the passing game in this century, All-Pro receiving performances from the 1990s might barely be top 10 worthy in the new era. Of the top 10 leaders in career receiving yards, only one never played a down in this century. By comparison, in the rushing game, that number is 5 out of 10. Receiving the football is a 21st-century pursuit, and the game's superstar wide receivers are better at it than ever.

Perhaps the best example of how the new pass-happy NFL has elevated the wide receiver position is Larry Fitzgerald of the Arizona Cardinals. Fitzgerald was the third overall pick out of the University of Pittsburgh in 2004. By his 10th season in 2013, he became the youngest player ever to reach the 11,000 career receiving yards mark.

Fitzgerald's exploits extended into the postseason as well. In his All-Pro season of 2008, Fitzgerald was instrumental in getting his team to the Super Bowl. In the playoffs, he caught 30 passes for 546 yards and seven touchdowns, breaking the records of the great Jerry Rice in all three categories. The Cardinals lost the Super Bowl to Pittsburgh. Fitzgerald has played in eight Pro Bowls, including a stretch where he was voted to the game seven years in a row.

Larry Fitzgerald

You do not have to be a first-round pick like Fitzgerald to have success as an NFL wideout. Central Florida's Brandon Marshall is the perfect case in point. The Denver Broncos drafted Marshall out of the University of Central Florida (UCF) in the fourth round in 2006. He did not play much in his rookie season, but in 2007, his career took off. Marshall had the first of seven consecutive 1,000 receiving yard seasons that year, including three straight 100-catch seasons with Denver. During a game against Indianapolis in 2009, Marshall set the NFL record for catches in a single game with 21. Despite Pro Bowl seasons in 2008 and 2009, the Broncos traded Marshall to Miami before the 2010 season.

Marshall played two seasons in Miami before being traded to Chicago in 2012, where he had a career season with 118 catches for 1,508 yards. He was voted All-Pro and made the fourth of his five Pro Bowl appearances. He was traded to the New York Jets in 2015.

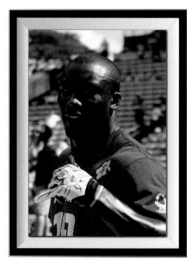

Brandon Marshall

In 2015, Antonio Brown of the Pittsburgh Steelers led the NFL in catches, the second consecutive season in which he was first in the league in this category. This is a pretty good result given that Brown was a 2010 sixth round draft pick out of Central Michigan, where he had walked on to the team.

Besides blossoming into a great receiver, Brown showed his skills as a punt returner. In 2011, he became the only player ever to rack up 1,000 yards in both returns and receptions in the same season. That year he went to the first of four Pro Bowls as a punt returner. In 2013 to 2015, he was selected as a receiver. 2014 was his best season, when a league leading 129 catches led to Brown winning the AFC Offensive Player of the Year. In 2015 Brown caught 136 and set a record by becoming the first player to ever have consecutive seasons with more than 125 receptions.

Dez Bryant knows a thing or two about breaking records. At Oklahoma State, he set a school record for receiving yards in a game by a freshman with 155. The following year he was a consensus All-American. After the following season, he left college to enter the 2010 NFL draft, where the Dallas Cowboys picked him in the first round.

Bryant is a two-time Pro Bowler, including his All-Pro selection in 2014, when he led the NFL in touchdown catches with 16. This was Bryant's third consecutive 1,000 receiving yard season.

Antonio Brown

THE TACKLERS

Scoring is only half the battle in the NFL, and on the other side of the ball are the defenders who try to disrupt the offense. None do it better than DE J.J. Watt. Drafted in 2011 by the Houston Texans, Watt is the most dominant defensive player in the NFL. The defensive end has won three NFL Defensive Player of the Year awards in his first five seasons while being voted a four-time All-Pro. Watt is also the first player ever to record multiple 20-sack seasons, leading the league in sacks in both 2012 and 2015.

The man who prevented Watt from winning four straight NFL Defensive Player of the Year awards is Carolina's Luke Kuechly. In 2013, the linebacker was the youngest player

Dez Bryant

ever to win the award, at age 21. Defensive Rookie of the Year in 2012, Kuechly went on to become a three-time first team All-Pro. He also won the Butkus Award as the league's best linebacker in 2014. Kuechly led the league in combined tackles in each of 2012 and 2014. He also holds the NFL record for combined tackles in a game with 26 in a 2013 game against New Orleans.

Richard Sherman

Succeeding Kuechly as NFC Defensive Player of the Year in 2014, Seattle Seahawk's CB Richard Sherman is one of the league's most intimidating pass defenders. A four-time Pro Bowler, Sherman led the league in interceptions with eight in 2013. That season, he helped lead the Seahawks and their so-called Legion of Boom secondary to a win in the first of back-to-back Super Bowl appearances. In that second Super Bowl season, Sherman grabbed two post-season interceptions. In 2015, his peers voted him the top DB in the league and the second best defensive player behind Watt.

Defensive tackle Aaron Donald of the Los Angeles Rams was NFC Defensive Player of the Year after Sherman for the 2015 season. The Rams did not have a good year, missing the playoffs in their last season in St. Louis, but Donald was a bright spot on a very good defense. He made his second straight Pro Bowl, following up his NFL Defensive Rookie of the Year campaign in 2014. Donald has impressed despite a relative lack of size, playing at 6'1" and 285 lbs., more than 50 lbs. lighter than many of his opponents on the offensive line. It is his quickness off the ball that helped produce 11 sacks to lead all defensive linemen in 2015.

Aaron Donald

From Unitas to Brady, Grange to Brown, and Hutson to Bryant, these are the best of the best ever to play the game. But which of these players was truly the greatest? That is the subject of considerable, and very interesting, debate.

Text-Dependent Questions:

1. Who was considered by experts to be the prototypical NFL quarterback and was selected by the Indianapolis Colts first overall in the draft in 1998?

2. Which Philadelphia Eagles player, chosen in the second round of the draft pick, led the league in rushing touchdowns in 2011 and in rushing yards in 2013?

3. Of the top 10 leaders in career receiving yards, how many never played a down in this century?

Research Project:

Look up the players taken in the first round of the last 10 entry drafts. Prepare a report outlining which of these high picks have been a hit versus which were busts. Define your criteria for determining success (number of games played in the NFL, point production, all-star selections, awards, etc.). Based on the results, rank each team according to their first round draft success.

RANDY MOSS

EMMITT SMITH

JIM BROWN

BARRY SANDERS

PEYTON MANNING

CRIS CARTER

JOHN ELWAY

STEVE LARGENT   JERRY RICE   ROD WOODSON

DEACON JONES

PRO FOOTBALL HALL OF FAME

TOM BRADY

The Pro Football Hall of Fame is located in Canton, Ohio. The hall recognizes players and other contributors to American football who have had outstanding accomplishments in the sport. Since it opened in 1963, the hall has enshrined more than 300 members, a very small percentage of the total number of players and other contributors who have been associated with the game since its origin. Induction into the hall is the ultimate honor awarded only to the very greatest in the game. Only a maximum of eight people, including just six players, can be inducted each year. About 200,000 people visit the Hall of Fame annually.

Scan here to go to the Football Hall of Fame website.

CHAPTER 7

WHO'S THE G.O.A.T.? (GREATEST OF ALL TIME)

It is an argument that persists in many areas of the culture beyond sports—who is the greatest of all time—the G.O.A.T., the best, number one? Which is the greatest band of all time? The best album? The greatest movie? Who is the greatest actor? The greatest president? The attempts to quantify the G.O.A.T., however, are especially pervasive in the metric-rich world of sports, and football is no different.

In any sport, football included, the chief difficulty in determining relative greatness is comparing players across eras. Technological improvements, rule changes, and the lengthening of seasons and careers are just some of the factors that need to be considered when assessing players from one era to another.

For example, there was a time when a 1,000-yard rushing season was the benchmark for a great year for running backs. In the 1950s, the season was only 12 games long, so it took an average of more than 83 yards a game to reach that mark. Since 1978, however, there have been 16 regular season games played in the NFL, which means just 63 yards per game are needed, a fairly average number. A thousand yards just does not have the luster it once did.

In the passing game, 100 receptions in a season was once a highly regarded accomplishment. Before 1990, only three players had ever done it in the 70-year history of the league. In the 1990s, however, football became a passing game, and by 1996, 23 players had achieved 100-catch seasons.

This is not to say that statistics are not important. They are the lifeblood of sports analysis and the foundation for any good argument about the G.O.A.T. at any position. Stats just need to be viewed through the prism of the era in which they were accumulated and to be supported by other indicators that the player in question was truly great—just because someone has better stats does not necessarily mean he or she is the better player.

Offensive linemen and tight ends are important to every team as well, but the following discussion of football's G.O.A.T. is limited to four key positions: quarterback, running back, wide receiver, and defense. Let the debate begin.

QUARTERBACK

It is inarguably the marquee position on the team: quarterback. This player touches the ball more than any other and is therefore in a position to have the biggest impact on a game. And that is especially true given that the modern NFL is a pass first league. Few have made better use of all those touches than Peyton Manning.

In 2016, Manning, already the career leader in touchdown passes, also became the career leader in passing yards. On statistics alone, Manning is unparalleled. He appeared in a record 14 Pro Bowls. He also holds the record for most NFL MVP awards with five. That is, however, three more MVP trophies than he has Super Bowl trophies. After a win in 2007 with the Colts, he finally won a second Super Bowl with Denver in 2016 at age 39.

Before John Elway became general manager of the Denver Broncos and signed Peyton Manning to play there after Manning left the Colts, he was once the Broncos star quarterback. As the first overall pick in the 1983 draft, he had led the Broncos to back-to-back Super Bowls in 1987 and 1988, but they lost badly both times. Fifteen years into his career, it looked like he may never win one. But in the late 1990s, he again led the Broncos to back-to-back Super Bowls, this time winning both Super Bowl XXXII and XXXIII. He threw for more than 50,000 yards and 300 touchdowns on his way to the Hall of Fame, both top 10 all-time.

Elway eventually became a winner but not like Johnny Unitas, Joe Montana, and Tom Brady. Each won four championships in the postwar era.

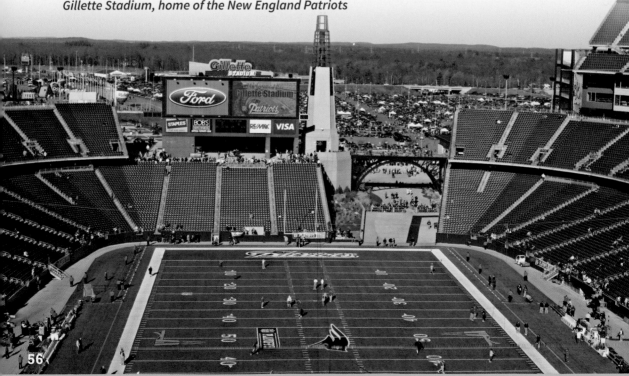

Gillette Stadium, home of the New England Patriots

Unitas was the first great quarterback. He led his Colts to three NFL Championships as well as the victory in Super Bowl V. Even though he played in a run-first, defensive era, Unitas still ranks in the top 15 all-time for passing yards and in the top 10 for touchdowns. The NFL voted Unitas as the best player the league had seen in its first 50 years.

Joe Montana won four Super Bowls with his San Francisco 49ers in the 1980s. He was not physically imposing, he did not have the strongest arm, and he was by no means the fastest player on the field. What he knew how to do best was win. He had the stats as well. Like Unitas, he also ranks in the top 15 all-time in touchdown passes and passing yards. Montana, however, was especially good when the games mattered most. He was uncommonly cool in pressure situations, going 4-0 (11 touchdowns, 0 interceptions) in Super Bowls. In fact, only one player in the history of the game has more playoff wins than Montana's 16, and that is Tom Brady.

Brady's Patriots were the model of consistency. In 2016, they won at least 10 games for the 13th consecutive year, and Brady was the centerpiece of that dynasty. He won those four Super Bowls, along with a couple of MVP awards along the way. He is top five all-time in both passing yards and touchdowns. Not only did he make great plays, but he also rarely made mistakes. Brady has been intercepted on only 2 percent of his pass attempts throughout his career, the second-best of all-time.

So who is the G.O.A.T. at QB? Most experts will say it comes down to either Brady or Montana. At the quarterback position more than any other, success is measured in wins and losses, and when it counted most, no one did it better than these two champions.

Joe Montana

Tom Brady

Peyton Manning

RUNNING BACK

At the running back position, there is really only one statistic—yards. So it should be easy to choose the G.O.A.T. at running back because no one has more career rushing yards (or touchdowns) than Dallas Cowboy Hall of Famer Emmitt Smith. But not so fast.

Longevity has to be factored into the equation here. Unlike quarterbacks, running backs do not last very long in the NFL. The position has the shortest average career duration of them all, at just over three years, so running backs with long careers make an impression in the record books.

Beginning in 1990, Smith was lucky enough to play for 15 years, five times longer than the average. So while Smith is an all-time great, three-time Super Bowl winner, and an NFL MVP, his greatest attribute was consistency over a long stretch. His career rushing record may never be broken, but Smith is not the G.O.A.T.

One measuring stick that levels the playing field is the rushing yards per game statistic. There are four Hall of Famers among the top 10 all-time in rushing yards gained per game: Jim Brown (104.3), Barry Sanders (99.8), Eric Dickerson (90.8), and Walter Payton (88). Smith ranks 16th.

Walter Payton played 13 seasons for the Chicago Bears from the mid-1970s to the mid-1980s. For 10 of those seasons, he rushed for at least 1,100 yards, an NFL record later matched by Sanders. Payton was a Super Bowl champion and a league MVP with a nose for the end zone. His signature was leaping over linemen at the goal line and going airborne to score touchdowns. Only Smith has more career yards.

Emmitt Smith

Eric Dickerson

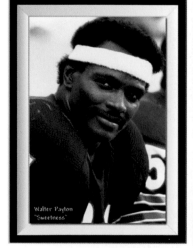

Walter Payton

With his signature goggles, Eric Dickerson was hard to miss on the field, unless you were a defender. Dickerson exploded into the league with the L.A. Rams in 1983, setting a rookie rushing record with 1,808 yards. The next year, Dickerson set another record, rushing for 2,105 yards for the season. Both records still stand. He would, however, play only 10 seasons due to chronic injuries. He never made it to a Super Bowl. Dickerson is seventh on the all-time rushing yard list.

Barry Sanders may have been the most elusive player in the history of the game. Sanders had to be great to gain his yards because half of his Detroit Lion teams of the 1990s were not. The defense keyed on Sanders on every series, yet he still ran for more than 15,000 yards in his career. Sanders never played in the Super Bowl, as his teams won only one playoff game. After his 10th season, he decided to stop. Sanders walked away from football at the height of his powers. Only Smith and Payton have more career yards.

Like Sanders, Jim Brown quit football (to pursue acting), while he was still one of the game's very best players. The stats paint a clear picture. Brown led the NFL in rushing eight times, which is a record. He went to nine Pro-Bowls. He scored 106 rushing touchdowns, fifth all-time. He is ninth all-time in yardage. He only played nine seasons, all in Cleveland. He led the Browns to the NFL Championship in 1964. Because he cut his career short, Brown is not at the top of the statistical heap. Those who watched him play or tried to tackle him, however, have no doubt who was the best. In 1999, *Sporting News* magazine ranked Brown as the G.O.A.T. at any position.

Levi's Stadium, home of the San Francisco 49ers

WIDE RECEIVER

For most experts, the conversation about who is the G.O.A.T. at the wide receiver position begins and ends with 49er legend Jerry Rice. Rice is the position's all-time leader in every significant category—catches, yards, and touchdowns—and it is not even close. He was a 10-time All-Pro, 3-time Super Bowl champion, and a Super Bowl MVP.

Rice was never the fastest or the strongest, but longtime Viking and Cardinal head coach Dennis Green once declared Rice to be "the best route runner I've ever seen." Rice also had a reputation as a great blocker, doing everything that his position required at the highest level. He scored more touchdowns than anyone in the history of the sport, with 208.

Cris Carter played his entire career in the shadow of Rice, which is why the Hall of Famer is sometimes overlooked as an all-time great player. Carter entered the league two years after Rice and retired two years before Rice did. At the time of his retirement in 2002, however, Carter was second all-time only to Rice in total catches and touchdown catches. His first NFL head coach in Philadelphia, Buddy Ryan, famously complained about Carter, "All he does is catch touchdown passes." He still ranks in the top four on both those lists and is top 10 in receiving yards as well.

FirstEnergy Stadium, home of the Cleveland Browns

The man who bumped Carter down on the all-time TD reception list was his teammate with the Vikings for four years, Randy Moss. Throughout his career, Moss was a vertical threat, feared for his potential to break away from defenses with his blazing speed and score on any play. Beginning in his rookie season in Minnesota, Moss routinely torched defenses for big plays. He was traded to Oakland in 2005 and then to the Patriots in 2007 when he caught 23 touchdown passes from Tom Brady, the most ever in a single season. Moss played in two Super Bowls, but his team lost both games. Only Rice has caught more touchdowns than Moss all-time, and he is top three in career receiving yardage as well.

Steve Largent broke in with Seattle in 1976, before rule changes protecting quarterbacks and restricting defensive backs turned the league pass happy. Because of this, he ranks just 16th in career receiving yards and 27th in catches. When he retired in 1989, however, he did so as the most prolific receiver ever to play to that point. His totals were all NFL records. Very few players can say they retired as the all-time leader in their sport at any position. That's how good Largent was. By the way, his 100 touchdown catches are still seventh best all-time.

That 100th touchdown is a big part of Largent's legacy because of the significance of the then record-setting total. For 40 years, the record was 99, set by the Packer's Don Hutson. Here is some perspective on that number: Hutson retired in 1945. At that time, his total was 67 more than his nearest rival, the Rams' Jim Benton. Benton retired two years later with 45 touchdown catches. Hutson had no peers when he played. More than 20 percent of all his catches were for touchdowns. Moss' percentage is 15.9 percent. It took Largent nearly 200 games to do what Hutson did in 116. For these reasons, the G.O.A.T. at wide receiver is not always a unanimous choice.

Jerry Rice

Cris Carter

Randy Moss

DEFENSE

Defensive backs primarily impact only the passing game, so in the discussion of the G.O.A.T. on their side of the ball, they usually come up short. Players like Rod Woodson, Deion Sanders, Paul Krause, and Ed Reed are mentioned, but then the discussion turns to the men up front. Defensive linemen and linebackers are the positions at which those considered to be the game's greatest are found.

Amongst these, New York Giants' linebacker Lawrence Taylor stands tallest. Taylor came out of North Carolina in 1981 and hit the league like a wrecking ball. Sacks were not an official stat until his second season, but he had 9.5 as a rookie, terrorizing quarterbacks at every turn. He got 132.5 more in his 13-year career for a combined number of 142, which would make him fifth all-time (officially he is ranked 11th). He was a 10-time All-Pro and a three-time Defensive Player of the Year and won two Super Bowls. The Raider's Hall of Fame head coach John Madden said, "Lawrence Taylor, defensively, has had as big an impact as any player I've ever seen." He is widely considered to be the G.O.A.T. to play defense.

Before Taylor, the man most considered (and some still do) to be the best linebacker of all time is Chicago's Dick Butkus. He is one of the most ferocious tacklers ever to roam the gridiron. In 1970, *Sports Illustrated* magazine dubbed him "The Most Feared Man in the Game." No one knows how many sacks Butkus had as his nine-year career ended in 1973, but the six-time All-Pro had a penchant for ripping the ball away from quarterbacks and ball carriers alike. He recovered 27 fumbles in his career, the sixth most in history. Despite Butkus' prowess, his Bear teams were mostly terrible, and he never played a single playoff game.

As Butkus' career was ending, over in Pittsburgh, the arrival of defensive tackle Joe Greene helped to change the fortunes of that franchise. Greene was drafted by the Steelers in 1969 and quickly got to the task of showing the league why his college nickname was Mean Joe Greene. Greene was Defensive Rookie of the Year and would also win two Defensive Player of the Year

MetLife Stadium, home of the New York Jets and Giants

awards in his 12-year Hall of Fame career. The team had not made the playoffs in 21 years when Greene arrived. That streak ended in 1972 as the Steelers evolved into one of the NFL's great dynasties. They made the playoffs every year through 1979, including reaching and winning four Super Bowls. The five-time All-Pro was the leader of the Steelers vaunted Steel Curtain defense.

While Greene dominated the interior of the defensive line, Philadelphia Eagles and Green Bay Packers star Reggie White made his living coming off the end at opposing quarterbacks. White played 16 NFL seasons from 1985 to 2000 and was voted to the Pro Bowl 13 times. He had nine straight seasons with at least 10 quarterback sacks, an NFL record. He racked up a number 2 all-time 198 sacks in his Hall of Fame career, most of those with the Eagles. But his biggest impact came as a leader on the Packer teams of the late 1990s. White and the Packers went to back-to-back Super Bowls in 1997 and 1998, winning the first one. The year they won the Super Bowl, White was Defensive Player of the Year.

White was prolific at sacking the quarterback, but the pass rusher who struck the most fear in the hearts of opposing quarterbacks was David "Deacon" Jones. In the 1960s, Jones and his Fearsome Foursome defensive linemates dominated games for the Los Angeles Rams. He is credited with coining the term sack for tackling quarterbacks, likening it to putting them in a burlap sack and hitting it with a baseball bat. Sacks were not kept as a stat by the league when Jones played, but he is unofficially believed to have had 173.5 in his 14-year career, which would be third all-time. Jones was also adept at chasing down ball carriers from sideline to sideline. He went to eight Pro Bowls and was a five–time All-Pro and a two-time Defensive Player of the Year in his Hall of Fame career.

Dick Butkus

Lawrence Taylor

Deacon Jones

Career Snapshots

Quarterbacks

#12 TOM BRADY 2000-Present

Career passing yards - 53,288
Career passing TDs - 392
Completion percentage - 63.5%

#18 PEYTON MANNING 1998-Present

Career passing yards - 69,991
Career passing TDs - 530
Completion percentage - 65.5%

#7 JOHN ELWAY 1983-98

Career passing yards - 51,475
Career passing TDs - 300
Completion percentage - 56.9%

#16 JOE MONTANA 1979-94

Career passing yards - 40,551
Career passing TDs - 273
Completion percentage - 63.2%

#19 JOHNNY UNITAS 1956-73

Career passing yards - 40,239
Career passing TDs - 290
Completion percentage - 54.6%

Running Backs

#22 EMMITT SMITH 1990-2004

Career rushing yards - 18,355
Career rushing TDs - 164
Average yards per carry - 4.2

#20 BARRY SANDERS 1989-98

Career rushing yards - 15,269
Career rushing TDs - 99
Average yards per carry - 5.0

#29 ERIC DICKERSON 1983-93

Career rushing yards - 13,259
Career rushing TDs - 90
Average yards per carry - 4.4

#34 WALTER PAYTON 1975-87

Career rushing yards - 16,726
Career rushing TDs - 110
Average yards per carry - 4.4

#32 JIM BROWN 1957-65

Career rushing yards - 12,312
Career rushing TDs - 106
Average yards per carry - 5.2

*All the above athletes are members of the Hall of Fame

Wide Receivers

#84 RANDY MOSS 1998–2012

Career receiving yards - 15,292
Career receiving TDs - 156
Career receptions - 982

#80 JERRY RICE 1985–2004

Career receiving yards - 22,895
Career receiving TDs - 197
Career receptions - 1,549

#80 CRIS CARTER 1987–2002

Career receiving yards - 13,899
Career receiving TDs - 130
Career receptions - 1,101

#80 STEVE LARGENT 1976–89

Career receiving yards - 13,089
Career receiving TDs - 100
Career receptions - 819

#14 DON HUTSON 1935–45

Career receiving yards - 7,991
Career receiving TDs - 99
Career receptions - 488

Defense

#92 REGGIE WHITE 1985–2000

Career sacks - 198
Career tackles - 1,112
Career interceptions - 3

#56 LAWRENCE TAYLOR 1981–93

Career sacks - 132.5
Career tackles - 1,088
Career interceptions - 9

#75 JOE GREENE 1969–81

Career sacks - 66
Career interceptions - 1
Career fumble recoveries - 16

#75 DEACON JONES 1969–81

Career Sacks - 173.5
Career interceptions - 2
Career fumble recoveries - 15

#51 DICK BUTKUS 1965–73

Career tackles - 1,020
Career interceptions - 22
Career fumble recoveries - 27

Words to Understand:

prominence: the state of being important, well known, or noticeable

cumulative: increasing or becoming better or worse over time through a series of additions

phenomenon: someone or something that is very impressive or popular, especially because of an unusual ability or quality

CHAPTER

THE FUTURE OF FOOTBALL

The current **prominence** of football on the American sports landscape would have been difficult for anyone to predict in the 1950s. Baseball was truly America's pastime, its passion, in fact. But by the 1970s, that was changing. When the very first Harris poll was conducted in 1985, it asked sports fans to name their favorite sport, and the NFL beat baseball 24 to 23 percent. That gap has grown significantly over the years.

In a 2014, the Harris poll was conducted for the 30th straight year, and for the 30th straight year, pro football was the most popular sport. The margin by which the NFL topped the results had widened, however—35 percent of fans named it their favorite sport versus just 14 percent for runner-up baseball. Football has enjoyed a remarkable run of increasing popularity, and all signs point to this popularity continuing to soar.

What has turned NFL football into the most popular sport in America? There are many theories, most with some key things in common.

APPOINTMENT TELEVISION

With its short, 16-game schedule, every game of the NFL season matters. Unlike baseball, where with 162 games it is easy to not pay attention to a Tuesday-night game in late July, all NFL games garner a spotlight. The NFL plays its games primarily on Sunday afternoons, and NFL game day has become a staple of the sports-viewing public in households across the country for three generations. Neighbors and friends gather at each other's homes on autumn Sundays to watch the local team each week. Every game on the schedule is an event, a must-see spectacle, and true appointment television.

PUTTING THE NATIONAL IN NFL

The NFL also holds real national appeal. From the mid-1990s through the turn of the century, the league expanded and moved teams to gain wider geographic appeal. Teams in Phoenix, Arizona; Nashville, Tennessee; Charlotte, North Carolina; and Jacksonville, Florida, greatly increased the NFL's presence in the South. No matter what television market in the country you choose, it has a "local" team whose games it televises every week, even if that team plays hundreds of miles away.

TV stations in Billings, Montana, show every Seattle Seahawks game, despite the fact that the team plays more than 800 miles away. With broadcast rights controlled by the league, the NFL TV contract has made the game a national sport. Everybody has a designated "home" team. And if you move away from your hometown to a part of the country where they do not show your team's games, the NFL offers a satellite TV package that allows fans to buy the right to watch any game from any part of the country.

FANTASY IS A REALITY

Perhaps the single element that has cemented the league's status as the most popular in America is the rise of fantasy football. The game comes in many varieties, but in all of them, competitors select teams of actual NFL players to manage and then use their real game statistics to match up against teams managed by fellow competitors. Unlike rotisserie baseball, the statistics are not **cumulative**. There is a designated game window that corresponds with the actual NFL game week, and teams accumulate wins and losses much like the actual NFL teams do.

Fantasy football draft

Fantasy football had its following in the 1990s but exploded into a cultural **phenomenon** after the turn of the century with the prevalence of the Internet. Gone was having to wait for box scores in the next day's newspaper to see if you won your matchup. Real-time game statistics available literally at the fingertips of players via smartphones have made fantasy football a multibillion-dollar industry that the league has embraced. Fantasy leagues are now all run on online platforms with automated management and user-friendly interfaces. The NFL now mandates that fantasy statistics be shown on video scoreboards during games in all of its stadiums.

The NFL embraces fantasy football because it gives fantasy players a stake in teams and players that are outside their local market. A fan in Pittsburgh on a week where the Steelers are on a bye might have little incentive to watch the filler game the local channel is showing between the Patriots and Colts that Sunday. But if that fan plays fantasy football, his fantasy quarterback might be playing for the Patriots, and his fantasy wide receiver might be on the Colts, giving the game another level of appeal.

INTERNATIONAL APPEAL AND BEYOND

Fantasy football is played in countries all over the world, part of the growing global appeal of the sport. Actual regular season games are played in London, England, every season. The reality of an internationally based franchise is anticipated to be a matter of when, not if. What else does the future hold? Here are some possibilities put forth by the league:

- Improved media technology will make it easier for people all over the world to consume the game, perhaps giving rise to the first generation of international players.

- Technological advancements will change the way players are evaluated and how the game is officiated.

- New 360-degree cameras could be placed inside each player's helmet.

- The in-stadium experience will improve with smaller, more intimate stadiums offering multiple seating options and free-flowing digital media access.

- Real-time monitoring and assessment of head injuries through advanced helmet technology will protect players.

- A change in the "tough-guy" culture of the game will be more accepting of missing time for injury and of openly gay players.

No matter how profound or impactful any proposed or imagined change may ultimately prove to be, the league will continue to grow and thrive due to the star power of its players.

Wembley Stadium, London, UK

Lambeau Field, Green Bay

CenturyLink Field, Seattle

Lincoln Financial Field, Philadelphia

FUTURE STARS

One of the brightest stars of the NFL in 2016 is Indianapolis Colts QB Andrew Luck. Luck was drafted first overall in 2012 and has proved to be every bit the star experts predicted. Luck took over a 2-14 team and proceeded to lead them to playoff appearances in each of his first three seasons, making the Pro Bowl himself in all three seasons as well. He set a rookie record for most passing yards in a season with 4,183.

The Kansas City Chief's Marcus Peters had an impressive debut to his NFL career. In the very first snap of his 2016 rookie season, the CB caught an interception. In his next game, he returned another interception for his first touchdown. This was how the whole season went for Peters, who led the league in interceptions and was named NFL Defensive Rookie of the Year.

THE GAME OF THE CENTURY

Stars like Luck and Peters will be the ones the players who take the field in the decades ahead emulate and idolize. Those players might hail from places like Germany or Ghana and play for NFL teams based in London or Barcelona, Spain. Officials may access a replay from their 360-degree in-helmet camera to determine if they got the call right.

Given what the first 100 years of football have produced, it is impossible to predict just what might happen. Having eclipsed America's pastime decades ago, football is poised to be America's game for the 21st century.

Andrew Luck

Marcus Peters

Text-Dependent Questions:

1. Perhaps the single element that has cemented the league's status as the most popular in America is the rise of what?

2. Give three examples of some possible changes to the future of football that have been put forth by the league.

3. Who was drafted first overall in 2012 and has proved to be every bit the star experts predicted?

Research Project:

Create and manage your own free fantasy football league with friends through *http://www. CBSsports.com*, ESPN.com, or Yahoo.com. Keep everything organized and running efficiently, and gain a sense of what goes into running a team. Manage your players, and learn what opportunities you may have to make changes in your team as the season unfolds. Through this you will learn much about your ability to think ahead. Using periodicals and online data on your players, evaluate your team as a manager would do. Ask questions of yourself—what did you like and what did you dislike about the process, and how might you do things differently in seasons to come? Evaluate your efforts to consider if this is an ongoing project you want to maintain in seasons to come. Enjoy!

GLOSSARY OF FOOTBALL TERMS

blitz: when the defense tries to overwhelm the quarterback by attacking from an unexpected direction.

block: stopping an opponent from getting in the way of a teammate.

clock: the device that tracks game time. The game includes four 15-minute quarters with a 12-minute halftime. The clock continues after tackles on the field but stops on any incomplete pass, when the ball carrier runs out of bounds during the last two minutes of the half, or when a team or official calls a time-out.

cornerback: the defender whose primary job is to keep wide receivers from catching passes. Good cornerbacks are usually the fastest players on the defense.

defense: the part of the team that tries to stop the opposing offense from scoring. The defense can line up in any formation and may move in any way before the snap. Standard defenses include the 4-3 (four linemen and three linebackers), the 3-4 (three linemen and four linebackers), goal line, nickel, and dime.

defensive backs: defensive players who play away from the line of scrimmage, for example, cornerbacks and safeties.

end zone: the place where touchdowns can be scored, a 10-yard-deep area located at both ends of the field marked by the goal line and the field boundaries.

field goal: when a placekicker kicks the ball through the uprights, worth three points.

formation: how the players are arranged for an offensive play. For passes, the offense may use five wide receivers, or on short yardage plays, it may line up three tight ends and two running backs close together.

first down: the first play in a set of four downs, or when the offense moves 10 yards in four downs or less.

fumble: when a player drops the ball before being tackled. Either team may recover the ball.

goal line: the line that divides the end zone from the rest of the field.

huddle: when the offense or defense gathers together in a group to go over the upcoming play.

interception: a pass caught by a defensive player instead the intended receiver.

lateral: a toss backward to a teammate. There is no limit to the number of laterals in a play.

line of scrimmage: an imaginary line the goes across the field horizontally from where the ball is placed. Seven offensive players must start on the line of scrimmage, and the defense sets up anywhere on the other side. Forward passes must be thrown from behind the line of scrimmage.

man or zone coverage: how the defense tries to prevent the offense from passing the ball. In man coverage, each defender focuses on one offensive player. In zone coverage, each defender focuses on an area of the field. Many defenses use both strategies in combination.

officials: those who enforce the rules of the game. In the NFL, there are seven, and they wear black-and-white striped shirts: referee (the head official), the umpire, head linesman, line judge, side judge, field judge, and back judge.

pass: when a player (usually the quarterback) throws the ball to a player farther down the field. A team can pass only once per play.

pass routes or patterns: the direction an offensive player runs to try to get open and receive a pass, for example, a slam, post, curl, in, out, or streak.

penalty: a rule violation called by an official. Most penalties are 5, 10, or 15 yards.

play action: an offensive play in which the quarterback pretends to hand the ball off but instead passes.

play clock: a game clock that players can see past either end zone. It counts down from 40 seconds at the end of the play and to 25 seconds for game-related stoppages such as penalties. If the offense does not snap the ball before time runs out, they receive a 5-yard penalty for delay of game.

possession: when a player controls the football. For passes, the receiver must place two feet, or a body part other than the hands, on the ground before going out of bounds.

punt: when the punter kicks the ball to the opposing team. Most often this happens on fourth down when the offense likely won't make a first down.

receiver: an offensive player who is allowed to catch a pass, usually a wide receiver, tight end, or running back. Most of the time offensive linemen are not eligible receivers; however, if one lines up off the line of scrimmage and tells the officials before the play begins, he can also catch a pass.

run: when the quarterback keeps the ball or hands it off to another player after the snap. The goal is to gain yards with the help of teammates' blocking.

sack: when the defense tackles the quarterback behind the line of scrimmage.

safety: 1) when an offensive player holding the ball is tackled in his own end zone—it's a rare play that earns the team on defense two points and the ball via a kick; 2) a defensive secondary position. There are two kinds: free safety and strong safety.

snap: how a play begins. The center snaps the ball between his legs, most of the time to the quarterback, punter, or placekick holder.

tackle: 1) an offensive player who lines up on the outside of the line but inside the tight end or a defensive player who protects the interior of the line; 2) making a ball carrier touch the ground with anything but his hands or feet, ending the play.

tight end: an offensive player who lines up outside an offensive tackle. Some offenses use more than one on running plays when they need just a few yards. Tight ends both block or run pass routes.

time-out: when the clock is stopped between plays. Each team has three time-outs per half, and officials can call time-outs too.

touchdown: when a player carries the ball and breaks the plane of the goal line or if a receiver catches the ball in the end zone. It is worth six points, and the scoring team can add a single extra point with a kick or two points by getting back into the end zone from the 2-yard line.

CHRONOLOGY

1874 Harvard and McGill play the first "American football" game.

1880 Walter Camp introduces the line of scrimmage, where players line up on each side of the ball.

1920 Representatives of 10 teams meet in Canton, Ohio, and form the American Professional Football Association (APFA).

1922 The APFA changes its name to the National Football League.

1946 Kenny Washington signs with the Rams—he is the first black player in the NFL since 1933.

1958 "The Greatest Game Ever Played" makes Johnny Unitas a star and the NFL an overnight national sensation.

1963 The Pro Football Hall of Fame opens in Canton, Ohio.

1967 The first Super Bowl is won by the NFL champion Green Bay Packers over the AFL champion Kansas City Chiefs, 35-10.

1967 The NFL Championship game is dubbed the Ice Bowl, with wind-chill readings lower than –40°F

1969 Jet QB Joe Namath legitimizes the AFL by guaranteeing then delivering a win over the Colts in Super Bowl III.

1970 The AFL and NFL merge.

1976 Seattle, Washington, and Tampa Bay, Florida, join the league as expansion teams.

1982 A player's strike lasting nearly five months shortens the season to nine games.

1987 The NFL uses replacement players for three games during a player strike.

1993 A new collective bargaining agreement between the league and the National Football League Players Association (NFLPA) establishes a salary cap.

1995 The league expands for the first time in 20 years when Carolina and Jacksonville are added.

2001 The "tuck rule" helps Tom Brady and the Patriots beat the Raiders and go on to win Brady's first Super Bowl. The rule was abolished in 2013.

2002 Houston is once again an NFL city, getting the expansion Texans five years after the Oilers left for Tennessee.

2009 Pittsburgh and Arizona play arguably the greatest Super Bowl of all time, won 27-23 by Pittsburgh on a tiptoe catch in the corner of the end zone with 35 seconds left

Football Today With safety concerns over repeated head trauma in the sport on the rise, national participation in high school football dropped 2.5 percent since 2008. Officials at the governing body for high school sports in California predict that by 2019 high school football on a national level will be at a "critical juncture". While other factors certainly contribute to the overall decline, with awareness heightened at every level of youth football, the concerns will have to be seriously addressed.

FURTHER READING

NFL Editors. *NFL Record & Fact Book 2014.* New York: National Football League, 2014

Editors of Sports Illustrated. *Sports Illustrated NFL Quarterback (QB): The Greatest Position in Sports.* New York: Sports Illustrated, 2014

Puldutor, Seth. *Drew Brees (Superstars of Pro Football).* Broomall, PA: Mason Crest, 2013

Biskup, Agnieszka. *Football (The Science of Sports [Sports Illustrated for Kids]).* North Mankato, MN: Capstone Press, 2014

INTERNET RESOURCES:

Football Hall of Fame http://www.profootballhof.com

ESPN NFL: http://espn.go.nfl

NFL http://www.nfl.com

Pro Football Reference http://www.pro-football-reference.com

VIDEO CREDITS:

Pro Football Hall of Fame Video Tour (pg 54) https://www.youtube.com/watch?v=019e1TPQdSQ

The Immaculate Reception (pg 8) http://www.nfl.com/videos/pittsburgh-steelers/09000d5d81d278eb/The-Immaculate-Reception

The Hail Mary (pg 9) http://www.nfl.com/videos/nfl-films-presents/0ap2000000103138/NFL-Films-Presents-The-Hail-Mary

The Catch (pg 10) http://www.nfl.com/videos/san-francisco-49ers/09000d5d8205e603/The-Catch

The Drive (pg 11) http://www.nfl.com/videos/nfl-videos/09000d5d825e71b1/This-Day-in-Football-The-**Drive**

Wide Right (pg 12) http://www.nfl.com/videos/nfl-videos/0ap2000000213456/Scott-Norwood-s-miss-field-goal

Music City Miracle (pg 13) http://www.nfl.com/videos/tennessee-titans/09000d5d81d991bc/Music-City-Miracle

One Yard Short (pg 14) http://www.nfl.com/videos/st-louis-rams/0ap2000000147500/Kevin-Dyson-tackled-at-the-one

The Helmet Catch (pg 15) http://www.nfl.com/videos/new-york-giants/0ap2000000146973/The-Helmet-catch

QR CODES AND LINKS TO THIRD-PARTY CONTENT

You may gain access to certain third-party content ("Third-Party Sites") by scanning and using the QR Codes that appear in this publication (the "QR Codes"). We do not operate or control in any respect any information, products, or services on such Third-Party Sites linked to by us via the QR Codes included in this publication and we assume no responsibility for any materials you may access using the QR Codes. Your use of the QR Codes may be subject to terms, limitations, or restrictions set forth in the applicable terms of use or otherwise established by the owners of the Third-Party Sites. Our linking to such Third-Party Sites via the QR Codes does not imply an endorsement or sponsorship of such Third-Party Sites, or the information, products or services offered on or through the Third-Party Sites, nor does it imply an endorsement or sponsorship of this publication by the owners of such Third-Party Sites.

PICTURE CREDITS

INDEX

In this index, page numbers in **bold italics** font indicate photos or videos.